WITHDRAWN

HISTORY
★ V·I·P ★

BOUDICCA

BRILLIANT
BIOGRAPHIES
of the
DEAD FAMOUS

Paul Harrison

First published in 2015 by Wayland
Copyright © Wayland 2015
All rights reserved.

Editor: Annabel Stones
Designer: Rocket Design (East Anglia) Ltd
Illustration: Emmanuel Cerisier, Beehive Illustration
Proofreader: Rebecca Clunes

Dewey number: 936.2'04'092-dc23
ISBN: 978 0 7502 8848 4
10 9 8 7 6 5 4 3 2 1

Wayland

An imprint of
Hachette Children's Group
Part of Hodder & Stoughton
Carmelite House
50 Victoria Embankment
London EC4Y 0DZ

An Hachette UK Company
www.hachette.co.uk
www.hachettechildrens.co.uk

Printed in China

Picture Credits: Stefan Chabluk: p5, p24; Science & Society Picture Library:
p15 © Universal History Archive/UIG, p19 © Universal History Archive/UIG;
Shutterstock: p8 abxyz, p20 chrisdorney, p26 Mike Fialkoff, p27 Ian Woolcock,
p29 Vladimir Korostyshevskiy; © Ad Meskens/Wikimedia Commons p22.
Graphic elements courtesy of Shutterstock.

CONTENTS

Introducing
BOUDICCA

Boudicca is one of the most famous women in Britain's history. Quite possibly she is the only Ancient Celtic Briton that most British people can name. She is best known for her violent revolt against the Roman army; but what else do we know about her? And how much of what we know is actually true?

WHO WAS SHE?

FULL NAME: Boudicca — also known as: Boudica, Boadecia, Buddug

DATE OF BIRTH: Unknown

PARENTS: Unknown

SIBLINGS: Unknown

MARRIED: Prasutagus

CHILDREN: two girls (names unknown)

DIED: 60 or 61CE

Boudicca was queen of the Iceni, a Celtic tribe from what we now call East Anglia in the far east of England. Boudicca lived in the middle of the first century CE, but we don't know exactly when she was born or where. We believe that she was tall with gingery-blonde hair and was married with two daughters, but we don't know the girls' names. In fact precise details of Boudicca's life are hard to find.

The main reason for the lack of information is that the Celts had no written language. Instead, history was passed down through the generations by storytelling. If the stories were forgotten then the history would be lost. Most of what we know of Boudicca comes from two Roman writers called Tacitus and Cassius Dio. They were writing from the Romans' point of view, so they may have been biased in favour of the Romans. Fortunately the work of modern-day archaeologists can help to shed more light on this brutal period of British history and Boudicca's part in it.

WELL I NEVER!

Historians disagree about the origins of the Celts, but it is generally thought that they spread from central Europe in around 800BCE. The Celtic tribes settled in countries across Europe; from Spain to Turkey and as far north as Scotland. The Celts were war-like, but also traders and fine metal workers.

- Original Celtic lands
- Later settlements
- Migrations

EARLY LIFE

Although historians don't know a great deal about Boudicca's early life, they do have evidence of what daily life would have been like in Celtic times. From this they can imagine what life must have been like for Boudicca as she grew up. The Romans often liked to portray the Celts as wild and savage, but in reality tribes such as the Iceni had a very ordered way of living.

WELL I NEVER!

Boudicca's Iceni tribe was well known for its fine jewellery. A hoard of Iceni jewellery found at Snettisham in Norfolk between 1948 and 1990 revealed thick necklaces called torcs that both men and women would have worn. The largest torc was made of gold and silver and weighed around 1 kilogram!

Celtic people belonged to different classes; and boys and girls of the upper classes, like Boudicca, would have been educated. Children lived with their families until they were around seven years old and then were sent away to continue their education elsewhere – whether it was with a relative, friend or even another tribe. Being sent to these so-called foster-families was expensive and apparently it was more expensive to educate a girl than a boy. Boudicca would have stayed with her foster family for around seven years.

After completing her education Boudicca would have returned to her real family and prepared for marriage. Although we don't know when Boudicca got married we do know who it was to. Her husband was called Prasutagus, and he was the son of Antedios, the king of the Iceni. Boudicca would most likely have been no older than eighteen years old at the time of her marriage. She had two children that we know of – both girls. In some cultures not having boys would have been bad news, but for the Celts a female was able to rule so the lack of a son was not a problem.

★ Celtic ★ tribes

Roman historians listed 27 separate Celtic tribes in Britain at the time of the Roman invasion. The Romans never referred to them as Celts, but as Britons.

ROMAN BRITAIN

By 62CE the Romans controlled a vast empire. They thought of themselves as being sophisticated and educated, so to the Romans, Britain seemed a remote and dangerous place. However, tribes in Britain had been trading with the Greeks and other nations for hundreds of years. Britain was known as an excellent source of slaves and tin, both of which were in great demand at the time. So it was only a matter of time before Rome tried to add Britain to its empire.

Emperor Claudius

The ★ Roman ★ Empire

The Romans were originally a tribe from central Italy. They would go on to build an empire that, at its peak, stretched from Britain in the west to Iraq in the east. It was the largest empire the world had ever seen.

In 43CE the Emperor Claudius sent part of his army to Britain in a successful invasion. It is likely that Boudicca grew up while Rome was slowly taking over the country. The Romans had two ways of taking control. Firstly the well-trained Roman army took advantage of the fact that the Celtic tribes were not united or as well-equipped in battle. Secondly the Romans allied themselves with some of the major tribes, including the Iceni. They agreed that these tribes could keep their lands but they had to support the Romans.

By the time of Boudicca's marriage most of Southern England was under Roman control. The first cities had been built at what we now call London, St Albans and Colchester – the first capital city. Roman architecture began to replace the wooden roundhouses the Celts lived in and Roman coins began to be used. In Roman terms, Britain was becoming civilised.

WHO WAS HE?

EMPEROR NERO

Boudicca became leader of the Iceni when the head of the Roman Empire was Nero (born 37CE – died 68CE). Known as a cruel and ineffective ruler, he is famous for murdering his mother and his wife, and for failing to act when the city of Rome burned. He eventually committed suicide to avoid being murdered.

CELTS Vs ROMANS

Although the Romans are credited with great advances in technology and building, they were happy to borrow ideas from other people – even the Celts. Boudicca's world was very different to the one the Romans portrayed. The Iceni, like the Romans, lived in highly organised communities. They were primarily farmers who lived in small, scattered groups and were surprisingly advanced. They actually invented many things that the Romans took credit for!

Traditionally, many believed that the Romans built the first proper roads but this appears not to be so. Archaeologists have discovered that the Celts built straight roads made with proper foundations and cobbles. These good quality roads explain how the Romans managed to move around Britain so quickly when they first arrived. The Celts also invented a type of plough that was much better than the ones the Romans had been using.

Where there was a marked difference between the Roman world and the Celtic one was in the type of housing that people

TRUE or FALSE?

THE CELTS INVENTED SOAP.

false The first recorded mention of soap dates back to around 2500BCE on an ancient Sumerian tablet found in modern day Iraq. However the Celts are believed to have used soap – but to clean their clothes and not their bodies.

lived in. Boudicca would have lived in a roundhouse – as its name suggests a round building made of wood and mud with a straw roof. It had no windows and the floor was made of flattened earth. A fire in the centre of the house would have kept it warm, but would have made the home very smoky. This must have looked very basic to the Romans who built houses with under-floor heating, and two-storey apartment buildings for city living.

WELL I NEVER!

You can still visit the site locals call Boudicca's palace today. It stood on what is now called the Fison Way near Thetford – though historians believe that what is buried under the ground is an Iceni holy site (like a temple) and not a palace.

11

BOUDICCA *in* CHARGE

When Antedios, king of the Iceni, died, his son Prasutagus became the new king. In turn when Prasutagus died – sometime around 60CE – Boudicca, his wife, took over as leader of the Iceni. This was totally normal for the Celts, but was a completely shocking idea for the Romans who did not think women were capable of being in charge. This difference in opinion would lead directly to revolution.

The Iceni were the same as other Celtic tribes in their ideas of what women could or could not do. Women could lead the tribe, as Boudicca did, and become druids or even warriors. They did not need a man's permission to trade goods or to get divorced. These freedoms were not enjoyed by Roman women. In the 'civilised' Roman Empire woman were much less important than men and the idea of a female ruler was considered ludicrous.

WHAT THEY SAID

The women of the Celts are nearly as tall as the men, and they rival them also in courage.

Roman writer Diodorus Siculus commenting on Celtic women.

★ Other ★ female rulers

Boudicca may be the most famous female leader but she is far from alone – even in Britain. Cartimandua of the Brigantes tribe from what is now modern-day Northumberland wasn't just a warrior but a skillful politician who managed to trade with the Romans and hang on to power.

What struck the Romans as particularly barbaric was the idea that women could be fighters too. Boudicca along with other female warriors, had a fearsome reputation. While this earned the Celts grudging respect in some Roman circles it was a practice the Romans were keen to eradicate.

TREACHERY!

When Boudicca became queen of the Iceni, the Roman occupation of Britain was still in its early stages. Whilst some tribes had been practically wiped out by the Romans for resisting their rule, the Iceni had cooperated and so been broadly left alone. However, neither the Iceni nor the Romans really trusted the other and their relationship was soon to crumble in horrifying circumstances.

After the death of Prasutagus, half of his kingdom was left to his two daughters with Boudicca in charge. The other half was left to the Roman emperor, Nero – possibly as a way of proving the Iceni's loyalty.

However, the Romans ignored the claims of Boudicca and her daughters, probably because they did not believe women could be in charge. The Romans started enslaving the tribespeople and taking whatever goods and possessions they wanted.

The Romans justified their actions by claiming it was repayment for a loan given to the Iceni.

However this was not the end of Boudicca's troubles. She was publically flogged and her daughters were brutally assaulted. This cruel treatment was an inadvisable course of action for the Romans to have taken. Although Britain was becoming Romanised, it was still far from settled. The news caused shock and outrage as it spread through the Iceni territory. What Boudicca did about it is recorded in history.

★ How ★ we know

Publius Cornelius Tacitus (CE56–117) and Cassius Dio (CE150–235) are the two Romans who wrote about Boudicca. Historians trust Tacitus' version of events more because his father-in-law, Agricola, was the general responsible for the invasion of Britain so could provide Tacitus with accurate information. Cassius Dio was born nearly 100 years after the events he describes and people are unsure of where he got his information.

UPRISING!

Boudicca wanted revenge on the Romans for what they had done and raised her tribe in revolt. However it was not only the Iceni who rose up against the Romans. The neighbouring Trinovanti tribe joined the rebellion and it is quite likely that other tribes came too. Boudicca's rebel army may have been as big as 100,000 strong and the first place they marched to was the town of Camulodunum.

Camulodunum – or modern-day Colchester – had been the centre of the Trinovanti tribe. However, when the Romans took over, they threw out the Celts living there.

To make matters worse, the Trinovanti were forced to pay heavy taxes to fund a large temple to Emperor Claudius. By the year 60 CE Camulodunum was the closest the Romans had to a capital city in Britain. Unfortunately for the Romans, at the time of the rebellion Camulodunum had no fortified walls and had very few soldiers to guard it.

When Boudicca arrived the town fell to the rebels. Within two days Camulodunum had been burnt to the ground; the inhabitants massacred; and anything of value had been taken. The Roman soldiers had barricaded themselves inside the temple, but there were too few of them to resist Boudicca for long. The soldiers were killed and the hated temple destroyed.

TRUE or FALSE?

THE CELTS USED TO BEHEAD THEIR VICTIMS.

true No one is quite sure why the Celts beheaded people but it may have been for religious reasons. The practice was one of the many things the Romans considered to be barbaric about the Celts.

SHOCK DEFEAT

Whether she knew it or not, Boudicca's attack on Camulodunum had been well timed. While the Celtic rebels were destroying the town, most of the Roman army under the command of Gaius Suetonius Paulinus (known as Suetonius) were fighting in Wales. This was one of the reasons why Camulodunum had been so poorly defended. However, another part of the Roman army was now closing in on Boudicca.

The Roman army was made up of highly trained, well-equipped soldiers. The army was split into units called legions that were made up of around 5,000 soldiers plus a number of what were called auxiliaries. These were often soldiers on horseback, or cavalry as we call them.

Unlike soldiers in the legions, auxilleries were not Roman citizens but were from countries Rome had conquered. The Romans had great faith in the effectiveness

IN OTHER NEWS

EXTENDED EMPIRE

Between 58–63CE the Romans were also fighting against the Parthians (from modern-day Iraq) for control of Armenia, in Western Asia. The conflict ended with no clear winner. Finally, a compromise was reached between the two sides.

of their legions as they symbolised the strength and organisation of the empire itself.

After the attack on Camulodunum it was the Roman's IX (ninth) legion that marched on Boudicca's troops. However Boudicca was not to be stopped so easily. Her troops, fired by their success in destroying the hated Roman town, did the same to the IX legion. It was a great victory for Boudicca and a humiliating defeat for Rome. On hearing the news the Roman emperor, Nero, considered pulling his troops out of Britain; but Suetonius was now on his way from Wales to confront Boudicca.

★ Druids ★

The religious leaders of the Celts were known as druids. Both men and women could become druids, and they were highly respected members of Celtic society. Although very little is known about Celtic druids it was claimed that they would inspire their warriors during battles with chanting and spells.

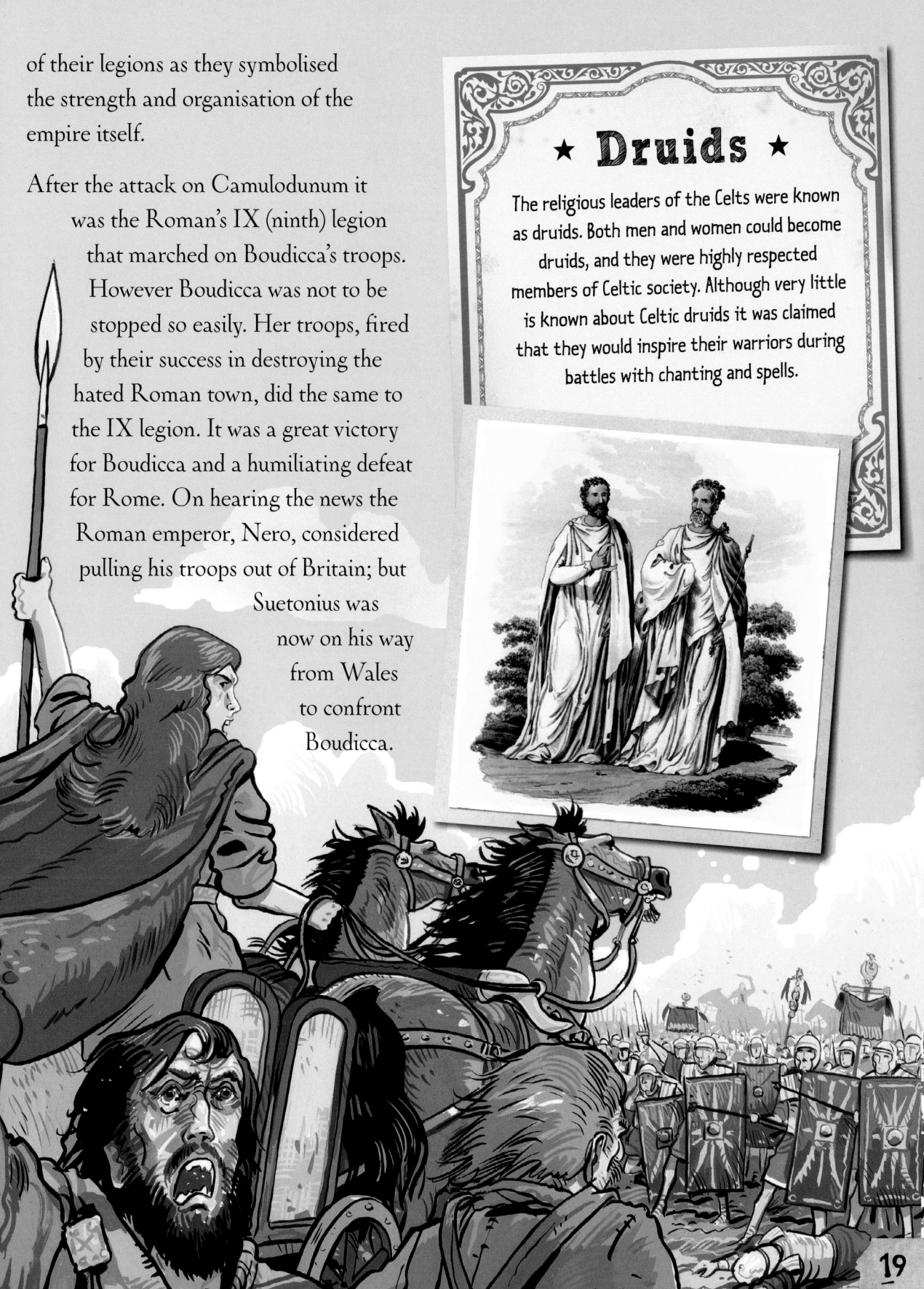

the UPRISING CONTINUES

After the defeat of the IX legion Boudicca moved her army to the south. She made sure to stay away from any Roman forts or army camps but made her way to the city of Londinium (present day London) instead. At the same time, Suetonius was marching his troops there from Wales.

Suetonius reached Londinium before Boudicca, but if the residents of the town were glad to see the Roman army arrive they were about to be very disappointed. Suetonius decided that it would be impossible to defend the poorly fortified town against Boudicca's rebels and marched his army away. Shortly afterwards

About 200CE, the Romans built a wall around Londinium. Parts of it can be seen today.

Line of ★ evidence ★

Archaeologists working in London and Colchester have found evidence of Boudicca's actions – a layer in the soil of burnt material. This is almost all that is left of the Roman cities.

Boudicca's army fell upon the town, which suffered the same fate as Camulodunum. The citizens were massacred and the buildings were pulled to the ground, one by one, and burnt. It was as if Boudicca was trying to erase all trace of the Romans ever having been there.

Boudicca then moved her army to the north and to the next city – Verulamium (modern-day St Albans in Hertfordshire). Like the previous two towns that Boudicca had razed to the ground, Verulamium was also poorly defended and stood little chance against Boudicca's revolt. It too was totally destroyed; its people – men, women and children – killed and its treasures taken. Roman control of Britain was hanging in the balance. The only person who could stop Boudicca was Suetonius – and he was on the run with his army.

TRUE or FALSE?

AROUND 70,000 PEOPLE DIED DURING BOUDICCA'S REVOLT.

true (possibly)... The figure comes from the Roman historian Tacitus, but archaeologists have not found any human remains at the sites of her attacks so the numbers cannot be confirmed.

THE END is NEAR

While Boudicca's army roamed where it wanted, Suetonius was desperately trying to find somewhere to fight that would suit his troops. Some historians believe he marched northwards towards the Midlands in his search. Boudicca may have realised that defeating Suetonius would rid Britain of the Romans. She turned her rebel army northwards and pursued the retreating Roman Army.

Suetonius

Boudicca's army and that of Suetonius could not have been more different. Boudicca's army was really a random collection of different tribespeople. A large number of them would have been warriors and these Celtic fighters were renowned for their ferocity and bravery. Coupled with this was the Celts' effective use of chariots. These lightweight battle chariots had one person driving them and one person on board to fight. They were effective on the battlefield and the Celts were highly skilled at using them. However much of Boudicca's army was made up of women and children and was not a highly disciplined fighting force.

WHO WAS HE?

GAIUS SUETONIUS PAULINUS (BORN ? – DIED ?)

Suetonius was more than just a general – he was also the Roman governor of Britain. He became governor in 58CE and later returned to Rome where he became a consul – the highest elected official in Roman government.

The Roman legions were highly trained and well-disciplined. The soldiers, known as legionnaires, wore body armour whereas the Celts had no armour and some tribes even fought completely naked. The legionnaires were professional soldiers and were highly experienced in battle. Suetonius knew that if he could find the right battlefield he stood a decent chance against Boudicca's forces.

TRUE *or* FALSE?

BOUDICCA'S CHARIOT HAD SPIKES ON THE WHEELS.

false **Pictures of Boudicca's chariot often show fearsome spikes on the wheels for attacking the enemy as she rode past. However there is no archaeological evidence that the Celts did this with their chariots.**

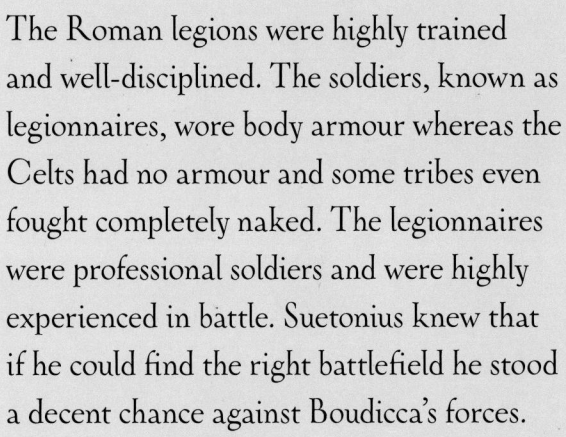

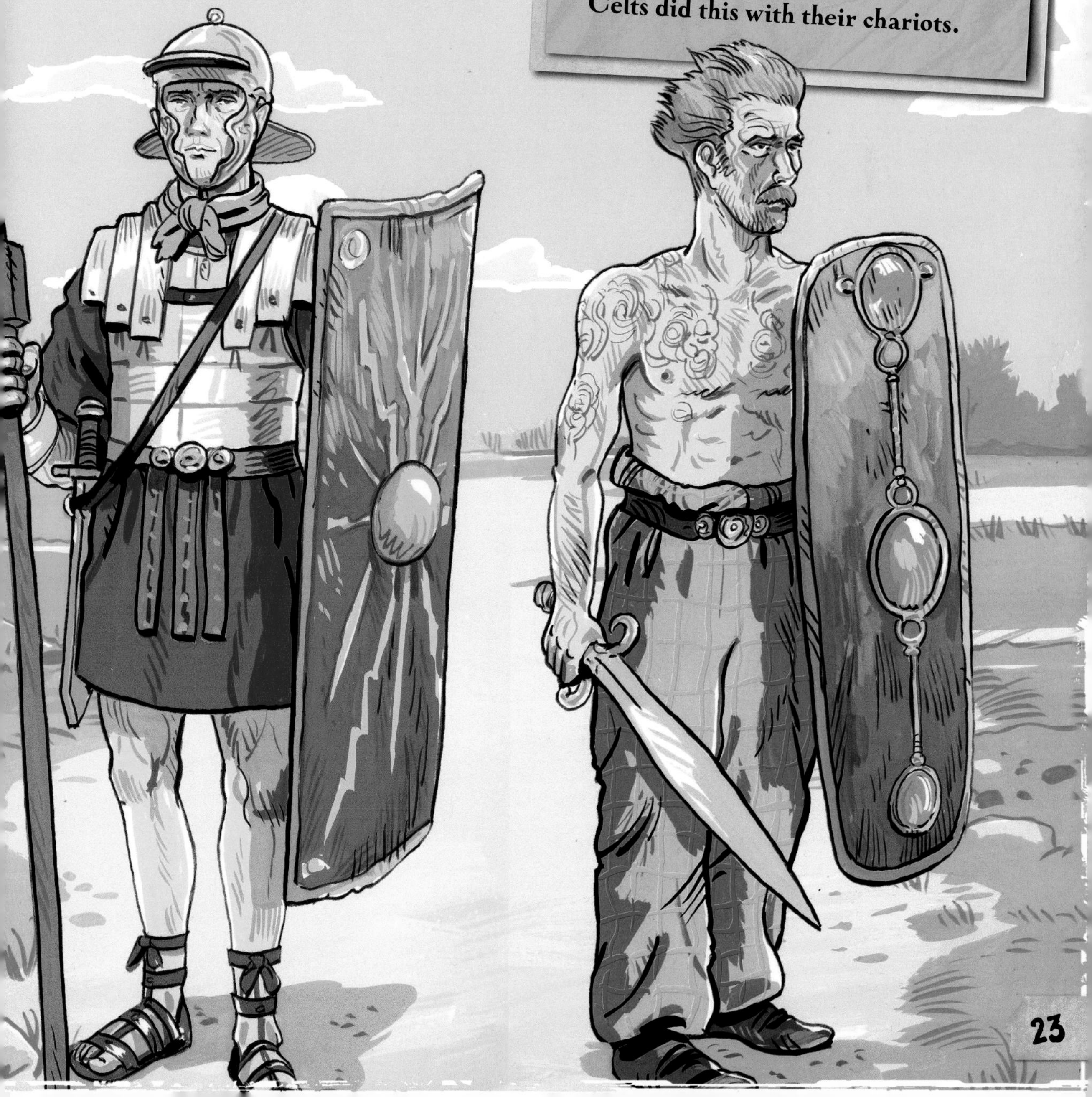

the FINAL BATTLE

By 61CE Boudicca had caught up with Suetonius. When she saw Suetonius's 10,000 strong force she must have felt very confident of defeating him with her larger army. However the Roman leader had chosen the battlefield very carefully and had given himself an excellent chance of victory.

Suetonius had positioned his legions in a narrow valley with a wood behind them. This was to stop the Celts from swooping around the Romans and attacking them from behind. Boudicca arranged her troops in front of the Romans and urged them on into battle. As the Celts advanced they were slowed by Roman arrows and javelins. Then the Romans charged in a wedge formation. This was where the soldiers arrange themselves into a triangle shape that was both aggressive and easy to defend.

The Celts turned to retreat but were caught up by their own troops behind them, who in turn were blocked from escaping by the wagons and animals they had left at the far end of the battlefield. The Celts were trapped and were massacred by the Romans. Boudicca's rebellion had been crushed.

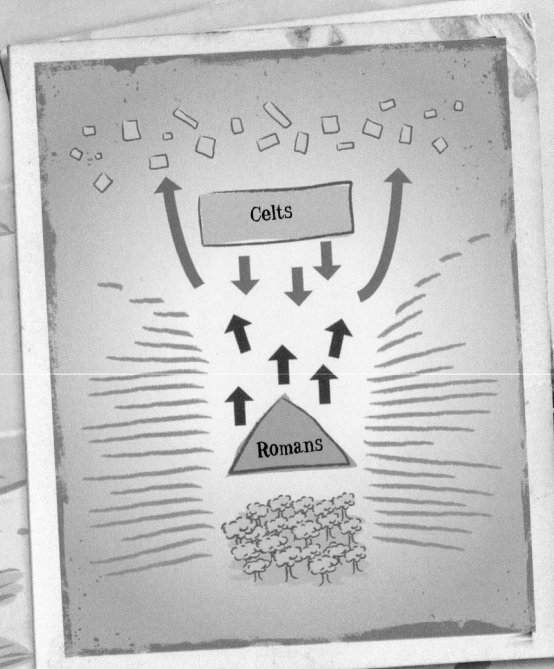

Although the battle has gone down in history as the Battle of Watling Street (the name of one of the main Roman roads), no one actually knows where it took place. Suggested sites have ranged from north London to the Midlands. However until some archaeological evidence is found we will never know for sure.

WHAT THEY SAID

It was a glorious victory that day, equal to our old victories. Some say that 80,000 Britons fell that day, with a loss to our soldiers of about 400, with a slightly larger number wounded.

Tacitus illustrates how decisive a victory it was for the Romans.

WHAT HAPPENED NEXT

The end of the Battle of Watling Street must have been a scene of chaos and carnage. The Celtic survivors would have fled in all directions, pursued by Romans on foot or by members of the auxiliary cavalry. Boudicca was among the survivors, but what happened next is something of a mystery.

Tacitus claimed that Boudicca poisoned herself after the battle to escape capture. It has also been suggested by some historians that she may have died from illness, or injuries suffered on the day. There is certainly some logic to Tacitus' claim. Boudicca would not have wanted to have been captured and left to the mercy of the Romans again – she and her family had already been badly treated once at their hands and this time it was sure to be worse. What neither Tacitus nor Cassius Dio mention is what happened to Boudicca's daughters. Tacitus states that they were with Boudicca at the battle but then they are never mentioned again.

The other mystery is what happened to Boudicca's body. One rumour claims that she was buried under what is now the area between platforms 8 and 10 of King's Cross railway station in north London. Although it's true that this is close to one end of the old Roman Watling Street, there has never been archaeological evidence to support this claim.

Some believe that Boudicca's final resting place is underneath King's Cross Station!

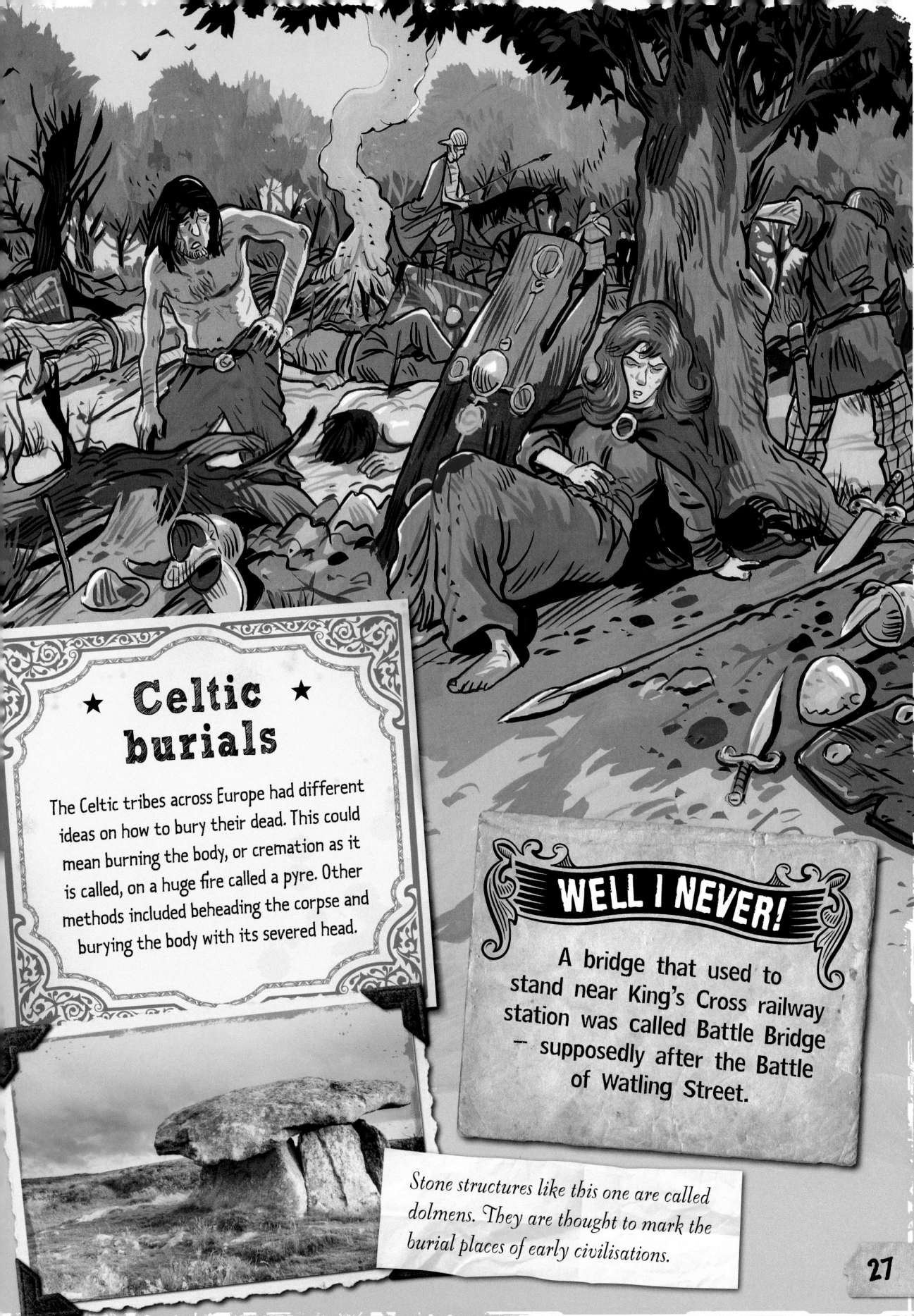

★ Celtic ★ burials

The Celtic tribes across Europe had different ideas on how to bury their dead. This could mean burning the body, or cremation as it is called, on a huge fire called a pyre. Other methods included beheading the corpse and burying the body with its severed head.

WELL I NEVER!

A bridge that used to stand near King's Cross railway station was called Battle Bridge — supposedly after the Battle of Watling Street.

Stone structures like this one are called dolmens. They are thought to mark the burial places of early civilisations.

BOUDICCA'S REPUTATION

For many years history ignored Boudicca. There was no mention of her during the Middle Ages – perhaps the idea of a strong female leader was out of fashion, or maybe the rulers did not want to spread tales of people rising up against those who were in charge. However the attitude to Boudicca changed during the Elizabethan period.

Following the death of Henry VIII and his son Edward VI, first Mary I and then Elizabeth I came to the throne. The idea of a woman in charge didn't seem so strange anymore. Having a strong female leader from history to look back to might prove that a woman could rule during difficult times. The fact that Boudicca was a warrior queen may also have appealed to Elizabethans as England was at war with Spain during much of Elizabeth's reign.

Boudicca became very fashionable again during the reign of Queen Victoria. The name Boudicca actually means 'victory' as does the name Victoria. There was also a trend at the time, for looking back at past glories – and Boudicca's tale was thought of as being a heroic struggle. A statue was raised in her honour outside the Palace of Westminster in London.

WHAT THEY SAID

In stature she was very tall, in appearance most terrifying, in the glance of her eye most fierce, and her voice was harsh; a great mass of the tawniest hair fell to her hips; around her neck was a large golden necklace...

Cassius Dio gives an idea of what Boudicca might have looked like.

Boudicca's ★ statue ★

At one end of Westminster Bridge opposite the Palace of Westminster stands a statue of Boudicca and her daughters in a chariot. Queen Victoria's husband, Prince Albert, paid the artist Thomas Thornycroft to build the statue. Although Thornycroft started designing the statue in 1856 it was not unveiled until 1902, the year following the death of Queen Victoria and long after the deaths of both Prince Albert and Thornycroft himself.

TIMELINE

55BCE	Julius Caesar invades Britain but does not stay
43CE	Emperor Claudius invades Britain
c. 40CE	The West Indies are settled by the Arawak tribe
44CE	Judea becomes part of the Roman Empire
47CE	The Iceni revolt against the Romans. The revolt is defeated, but the Iceni are allowed to keep their lands in return for promises of peace
c. 49CE	Camulodunum, the first Roman British town is started
c. 50CE	The Aksum kingdom begins in modern-day Ethiopia – it will last for hundreds of years
	Londinium is started
51CE	British Celtic chief Caractacus is captured after leading a revolt against the Romans
54CE	Emperor Claudius dies
	Nero becomes emperor
60CE	Prasutagus, leader of the Iceni, dies
	Romans seize Iceni land and possessions
	Boudicca is flogged and her daughters are assaulted
	Boudicca raises a rebellion and attracts support from other tribes
	The town of Camulodunum is destroyed by the rebels
	The IX Legion is defeated
	Boudicca destroys Londinium
	Verulamiun falls to Boudicca's forces
	First gospel of the life of Jesus is written by the apostle called Mark
61CE	Boudicca is defeated at the Battle of Watling Street
	Boudicca dies

GLOSSARY

archaeologist person who studies ancient human history

archaeology the study of ancient human history

architecture building design

barbaric uncivilised, not advanced

biased a point of view that favours one side over another

carnage killing on a large scale

druid a Celtic priest

emperor the leader of an empire

empire an area controlled by a single country

enslave to make someone a slave

eradicate wipe out

ferocity fierceness

fortify to strengthen a place against attack

impartial looking at both sides of a dispute or idea without favouring either side

javelin a type of spear

massacred when a group of people are murdered

primitive simple, not very complicated or scientifically advanced

Sumerian from the ancient city of Sumer in modern-day Iraq

revolt when people fight against those in charge

further information

BOOKS

Famous People Famous Lives: Boudicca by Emma Fischel (Franklin Watts, 2002)

The Story of Boudicca by Tony Bradman (Wayland, 2008)

Boudicca, Warrior Queen by Sian Busby (Short Books, 2006)

Horribly Famous: Boudicca and her Barmy Army by Valerie Wilding (Scholastic, 2011)

WEBSITES

www.museumoflondon.org.uk/explore-online/pocket-histories/queen-boudica-london/
A great site with information about Boudicca's revolt.

www.museums.norfolk.gov.uk/Whats_On/Virtual_Exhibitions/Boudica_Gallery_Trail/index.htm
Lots of artefacts from Boudicca's time, found in Norfolk.

www.theschoolrun.com/homework-help/boudica
Find out more about Boudicca with images, facts and a timeline.

PLACES TO VISIT

The Museum of London, 150 London Wall, London EC2Y 5HN

The Castle Museum, Castle Park, Colchester, Essex CO1 1TJ

Iceni Village Nature Reserve and Museums
Cockley Cley Iceni Village, Cockley Cley, Swaffham, Norfolk PE37 8AG

Boudicca's Palace Fison Way, Thetford, Norfolk

INDEX

More history titles available ❧ from Wayland… ❧

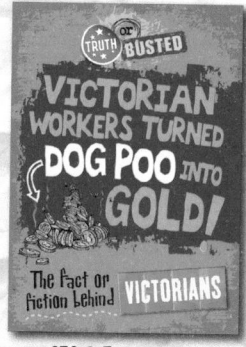